Marin City Memories

Marin City's pioneers speak about the early days of their unique community—created by war and kept alive through faith and determination.

Marin City Memories

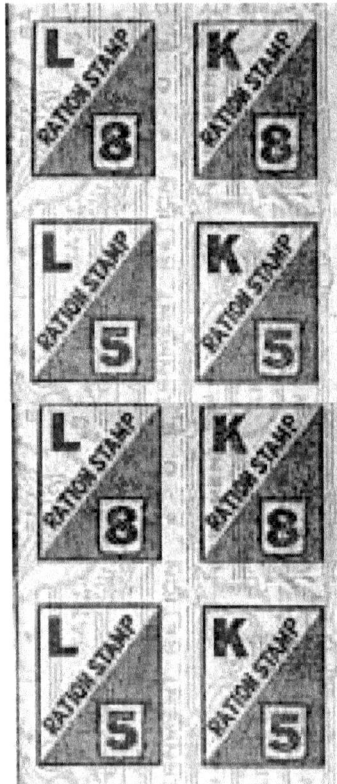

A Memory Book Project
by Marilyn L. Geary
for the
Marguerita C. Johnson Senior Center
Marin City, California

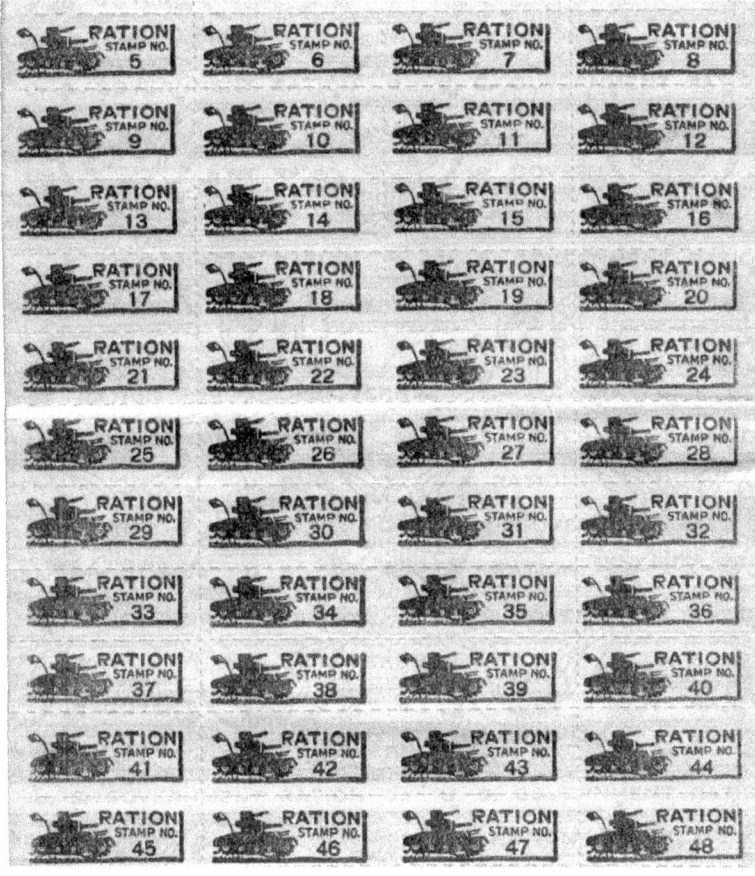

Funded by a
Community Arts Grant
from the
Marin Arts Council

Published in the
United States of America
by Circle of Life Stories
October, 2001

Marin City Memories

Introduction

In the early 1940's, the rural area nestled under high ridges just north of Sausalito looked much like the rest of Marin, rolling golden hills sprinkled with oak trees and dairy barns. A large shellmound area stood as a reminder of the valley's early native settlers, and only a few scattered houses dotted the rim of the crescent-shaped valley.

Then Pearl Harbor shocked our nation into war. W.A.Bechtel Company, awarded the contract to construct a shipbuilding facility in Sausalito, estimated that 15,000 workers were needed to keep the yard operating 24 hours a day. Almost overnight, the federal government changed this sleepy valley into what was called "a complete modern city" with 1500 light-framed houses and apartments, a school, a post office, an administration building, a cafeteria, a library, and other services for the Marinship workers.

Workers of all races and ethnic origin, recruited to work in the shipyard from around the country, moved with their families to the new town of Marin City. Many Black workers came from the South, from Louisiana, Texas, Arkansas, and Mississippi, where wages were low and the future limited.

Marin City Memories

The community was racially integrated, and the housing rented on a first-come, first-serve basis without regard to race. In April 1943, less than a year after Marin City was built, residents started the non-profit Marin City Council, Inc. (Tenant's Council) to provide community services. A newspaper kept all shifts informed of community happenings, and facilities served members regardless of color.

Although Marin City was well-integrated, prejudice was pervasive in the Bay Area craft unions. The chief shipyard union, the International Brotherhood of Boilermakers, Iron Shipbuilders and Helpers of America, refused to admit Blacks, and instead required them to pay dues to an auxiliary that offered lesser benefits than a full-fledged union membership. The Blacks at Marinship boycotted the auxiliary and refused to pay their dues. Their struggle eventually resulted in a victory to open the union to Black membership and a landmark California Supreme Court decision against racial discrimination in employment.

With the war won, Marinship formally closed on May 16, 1946. Although the shipyard work ended, many people stayed on, hoping for a better future in Marin City. But although the Black workers had earned as much money working in the shipyard as their Caucasian co-workers, they were trapped by discrimination from moving into other areas of Marin. By 1961, the original integrated community of 6,000 had dwindled to a largely Black community of 1,700.

Marin City had been quickly planned in three days as a temporary town. Materials essential to the war effort were conserved during the building of Marin City structures. Neglect over time made this temporary housing dilapated beyond repair. Those community members remaining after the war fought hard for permanent housing. Eventually in 1956, with the help of Supervisor Vera Schultz, Marin City was slated for redevelopment. Under developer James Scheuer's plan for renewal, the wartime housing and service buildings were torn down, new housing was built, and families were relocated.

Lengthy delays and plan changes left the promise of redevelopment largely unfulfilled. The commercial center, the post office, restaurant, drug store, library, laundry, and beauty parlor were torn down and not replaced. The Marin City Flea Market was held on weekends on the site of the old shopping center.

Over the succeeding decades, the community struggled to survive despite isolation and economic disadvantage. The many churches in the community played a significant role in binding the community together. In 1980 the Marin Community Development Corporation formed to boost economic development. A Marin City USA proposal was approved by the County in 1992, and the

Marin City Memories

Gateway Retail Center opened in 1996. Today new apartments and townhouses fill the bowl where the wartime housing once stood.

Some of Marin City's well-known landmarks have been lost. The Marin City Flea Market has been shut down, and Hayden's Market, the last locally owned retail business operating prior to the recent development, is gone. A unique structure from pre-World War II days is left to remind us of the area's early history. Built in 1907 by San Francisco lumberman Chandler William Burgess, this mansion sits behind dense vegetation on Donohue Street and houses a small private school.

With vast physical changes have come equally sweeping social and demographic changes. A recent survey determined that Blacks are no longer the majority in Marin City. Residents from a variety of ethnic backgrounds have moved into the new housing in the area.

As the community continues to transform and redefine itself, the voices of the past are fading. Many of Marin City's early pioneers are now deceased. In this book, community elders recall their experiences of Marin City during and after the wartime years. Their words bring us back to a time when the need to build warships created an instant city out of dairy farmland and urge us to remember that these pioneers' successful struggle to keep Marin City alive is a testament to their immense faith, strength and determination.

Marin City Memories

World War II Ration Stamps

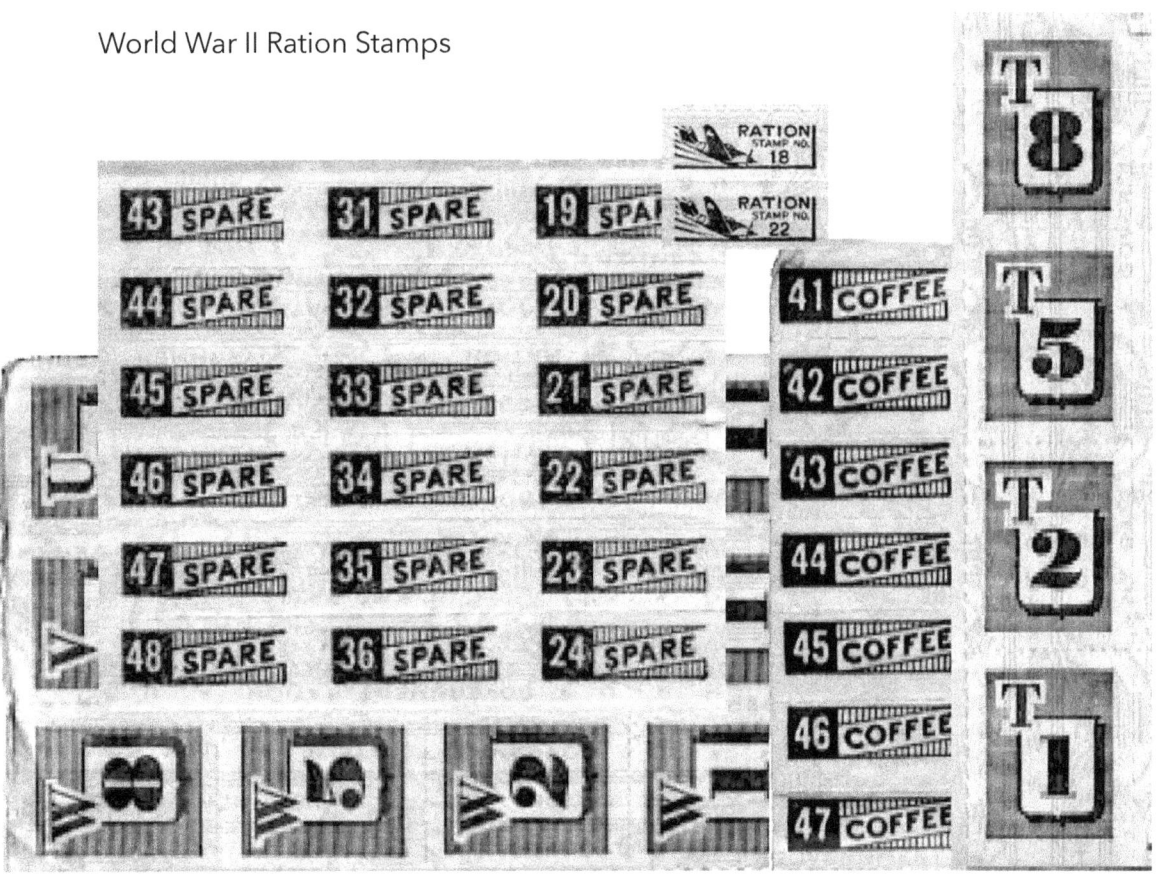

Marin City Memories

I came here to work in the shipyards. I was living in Baton Rouge and was working the daytime and studying welding at night at Southern University. Me and Elijah Beaucamp came out here to work. We had a friend on Post Street in San Francisco, so we went there first and then got a bus on Van Ness and came over here. We got off near where Big G was and walked up the hills to the dormitories. I knew I was going to stay as long as I could. I couldn't see no reason to go back home.

—Lee Sims

Marin City Memories

We came over on the bus, and we got to Sausalito, to Marinship itself, and my grandmother said, "This is where we get off." She thought that was Marin City, and we got off about where 3030 Bridgeway is located now. Then we didn't know where to go. We had all these suitcases. Then this neighbor came up, and he saw that we were looking perplexed, I guess, and he thought he'd better see if he could help. He asked us if we needed help, and we said, "Yes." We told him we wanted to go to the Hills' home in Marin City. He said, "Well, I live right next door to the Hills. I'll be very glad to take you over." So he bundled us up in his car and drove us around to the house.

—Betty Times

Marin City Memories

They were building Brice Brothers store when I came here. . . and grading out a road near where the Manzanita Center is now and building houses along that road. I helped to build the underpass between Marin City and Sausalito myself.

—Lee Sims

Marin City Memories

I took a bus out here, believe it or not. In the South there was only one seat in the back and two little side seats in the rear just ahead of the back seat. That was it for Black people. Even if there were (other) seats, you couldn't sit in them. I had a lunch that my wife had packed, and some lady that was sitting down held my lunch for me while I stood there. Finally I sat down on the arm of the seat that she was sitting in. When she got off in Texas, oh boy, I felt like I was crawling into a bed, just to sit down (laughs). Oh, it was really, really something, really. I'll never forget that experience. I still had a long way to go. I had to stand about three hundred miles.

—James Quiett

Marin City Memories

It was a beautiful place, but you know what? We had those little brown houses with the green top on them. I said, "They look just like turtles." Everybody said, "What's you mean?" And I said, "We don't have that back there." We didn't have houses like that in Mississippi. We had brick houses. Red brick houses and the windows were white. I said, "That's all I know about." But I came out here, and I said, "Look at the turtles with the green tops and brown around the sides*." But I come to like it.

—Nora Lee Condra

* The colors used on the wartime houses in Marin City were meant to camouflage the structures.

Welders - Edward T. Anderson - Elvin Barrow - Moses Beard

Marin City Memories

I thought I was going to a city that had lights and streets and stores. It wasn't like a city. I was from Texas. I'd been to Dallas and Longview. It wasn't like in Dallas and Longview. It was different. I expected better. I was very disappointed. But the longer I stayed here, the better I liked it. It grew on me. Finally we got a place to stay here in B3 — a one-bedroom.

—Wilma Hall

Welders-Theo & Vivian Barron-Jessie Berry-Thurman Burns

Marin City Memories

We kept looking and waiting for the Golden Gate Bridge because we thought it was literally gold. We were disappointed when we saw it. There was just the paint, and there was nothing golden about it.

—Thelma McKinney

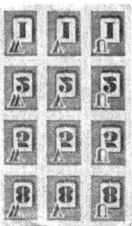

Welders - Lindsay Cage - Juanita Cobb - Otis Gaines, Sr - Hughey Griffin

Marin City Memories

I came to Marin City on July 17, 1944. I had a friend here, Melvin Smith, and he told me to come out here and get a job. I'd just been running around and I decided to come. They used to say that in California there was "money on trees as thick as oak leaves." I remember that I came on the train and got off in Oakland and took the ferry from Oakland to San Francisco. I walked down Market Street and caught a bus to Marin City. I would have left right then but Melvin talked me into staying. I didn't like it because it was so cold. I'd just left the South and you know how hot it is there. I remember I had on a white "flour sack" suit when I got off the train, and I almost froze to death walking down Market Street. The first thing I did was buy me some overalls. I got me a room in the dormitories (where Bayside School is now) and began working the next day. I had two jobs. I worked in the shipyards as a painter in the daytime and in the dormitories at night. I didn't intend to stay when I left the shipyard, but I ended up working in San Francisco from 1946 to 1977 when I retired. I've been here 36 years . . .

—Charles (Sport) Hodges

Welders-Ollie & Willie Hector-Leon Wade-Louise Howard-Thelma McKinney

Marin City Memories

We lived way up on the top of the hill near the water tank. There were times when the wind would be so furious that my children couldn't come through the door. I would always have to make sure that when they came from school that I was home so I could get them through the door. It's very windy up on that hill.

—Helen May

Welders-Louise McMichael-James Miller-Almeda & Buster Murray

Marin City Memories

I started work in the shipyard in 1942 and stopped working there in 1945. I was a chipper. I chipped steel. I made $1.04 an hour on the swing shift. The things I remember about Marin City are that things were a lot cheaper. Gas was about 13 cents a gallon and the price of a loaf of bread was 25 cents a loaf, but we had O.P.A. stamps.*

—Roscoe McIntosh

* Office of Price Administration ration stamps

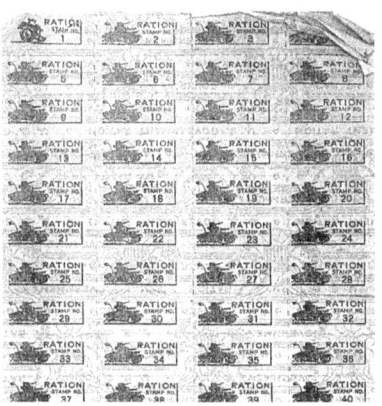

Marin City Memories

Welders-Mack & Louise Page-Helen Simon-Lincoln Simpson-Annie Small

Marin City Memories

We were recruited from Louisiana. They wanted people to work in the shipyards and my husband, Dan, came out first. He later sent me fifty $20 bills to come to California and I fainted right on the spot when I opened the letter because I'd never seen so much money before. I'll never forget it. They had to take me away in a Yellow Cab. (You know Black people weren't allowed to ride in Yellow Cabs then, but they put me in one to get me off the street, I guess...)

—Bea Hayden

Herb Wade, Sr. - Boilermaker - James Quiett - Chipper - George Dyer

Marin City Memories

I remember getting off the bus in Marin City and walking up the hill and almost falling down in the mud. I was carrying my daughter, Nita, and my suitcase. It wasn't what I was accustomed to, but it wasn't any worse. I knew that I would make this my home. Money was the incentive. We could work here and make good money. Me and my husband worked side by side in the shipyards. In those days, there were a lot of different nationalities here - Arabians, Egyptians, everybody. It was like a melting pot. We were just a bunch of people trying to make a living. There was no crime, no stealing -nothing like that. You could have your door wide open and no one would take anything...

—Bea Hayden

Chippers - Roscoe McIntosh - Clay Murray - David Smith

Marin City Memories

My brother was already a journeyman welder at Marinship, and I went down and put in an application. I was called and the first day on the job they had me in the double-bottom of a ship and I didn't like that. I didn't like the idea of working in the double-bottom of the ship. It was very dark, and you had to crawl around, and there was someone calling out to you where you should weld. I didn't like it at all.

—Thelma McKinney

Marin City Memories

There wasn't too many automobiles. People usually would ride the Greyhound Bus or the shuttle bus. That shuttle bus would run every ten minutes from the end of Sausalito to Marin City. They had a Greyhound station here. You could buy a ticket to anywhere in the United States so people would come in here on the Greyhound bus.

The shuttle bus was like a little school bus. It took about 15 or 20 passengers. It took about ten cents to go to Sausalito and back.

They had shifts, morning, swing and graveyard, twelve to seven. I worked the day.

—Frank Phillips

Marin City Memories

Everybody was making money. EVERYBODY was working. Young people — old people — people older than I am now were working picking up trash and sweeping and doing things like that. We worked 7 days a week, 24 hours a day building ships.

—Jesse Berry

A lot of people was working in the shipyard. They were working in shifts and sleeping in shifts. The guy who lived next door to my aunt about 12 people lived in that house, in a one-bedroom, but they all worked different shifts, and they'd come in to sleep.

—Mary Peoples

In September '43, most all the Blacks walked out because they wouldn't take us in the Boilermaker's Union. They had an auxiliary they wanted us to join, but we wouldn't join, so they got an injunction, and Judge Butler made us all come back to work. It was just about a day and a half. We came out that morning and came back the next day. The war was going on real heavy, and they really needed workers, one way or another.

—Frank Phillips

Electricians - Edward Janis - Austin "Tommy" Thompson

Marin City Memories

Before they tore down the war houses, there was a post office, there was a medical center, a cafeteria, drugstore, barber shop, beauty shop, Brice Brothers store, which was a supermarket, and then there was another little Mom and Pop's store. There was a wash house, the bus station. In fact, we had just about what Sausalito has.

—Helen May

Riggers - Willie Hector - Frank Phillips - Lee Oscar White

Marin City Memories

Grade School

The dormitories were where most of the early workers were living. The dormitories are now in the area where the Bayside School . . . is located.

—Betty Times

Marin City Memories

Admin Building

We never did have to go outside of Marin City to take our babies to have their shots. We had a place down there that you take your babies to get the shots. We had doctors come in here. The doctor come in once or twice a week. Then we had the post office and the police station, and we had the fire house here on the corner where Cornerstone Church of God in Christ is. We had houses stuck all around on the hill.

—Nora Lee Condra

Marin City Memories

When I moved out of the house with my brother-in-law and sister-in-law, we moved to a one-bedroom. From a one-bedroom, we moved to a two-bedroom. From a two-bedroom we moved to a house that was on top of the hill. And that's where we stayed. The bigger our family got, the bigger house we went in. And then finally they started tearing down everything.

—Wilma Hall

Painters - Charles "Sport" Hodges - Otis Williams

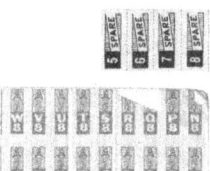

Marin City Memories

They were little brown houses, pretty modern. They had windows that weren't sliding windows. You had to push them out. They were kind of more like cabins than they were houses, but the structure was the same as any other house. We had a living room, we had two bedrooms and a bathroom, a little dining area and a kitchen, and they were comfortable.

—Helen May

 Other Workers - Cecil Bates - Frank Crock - Melvin Dennis

Marin City Memories

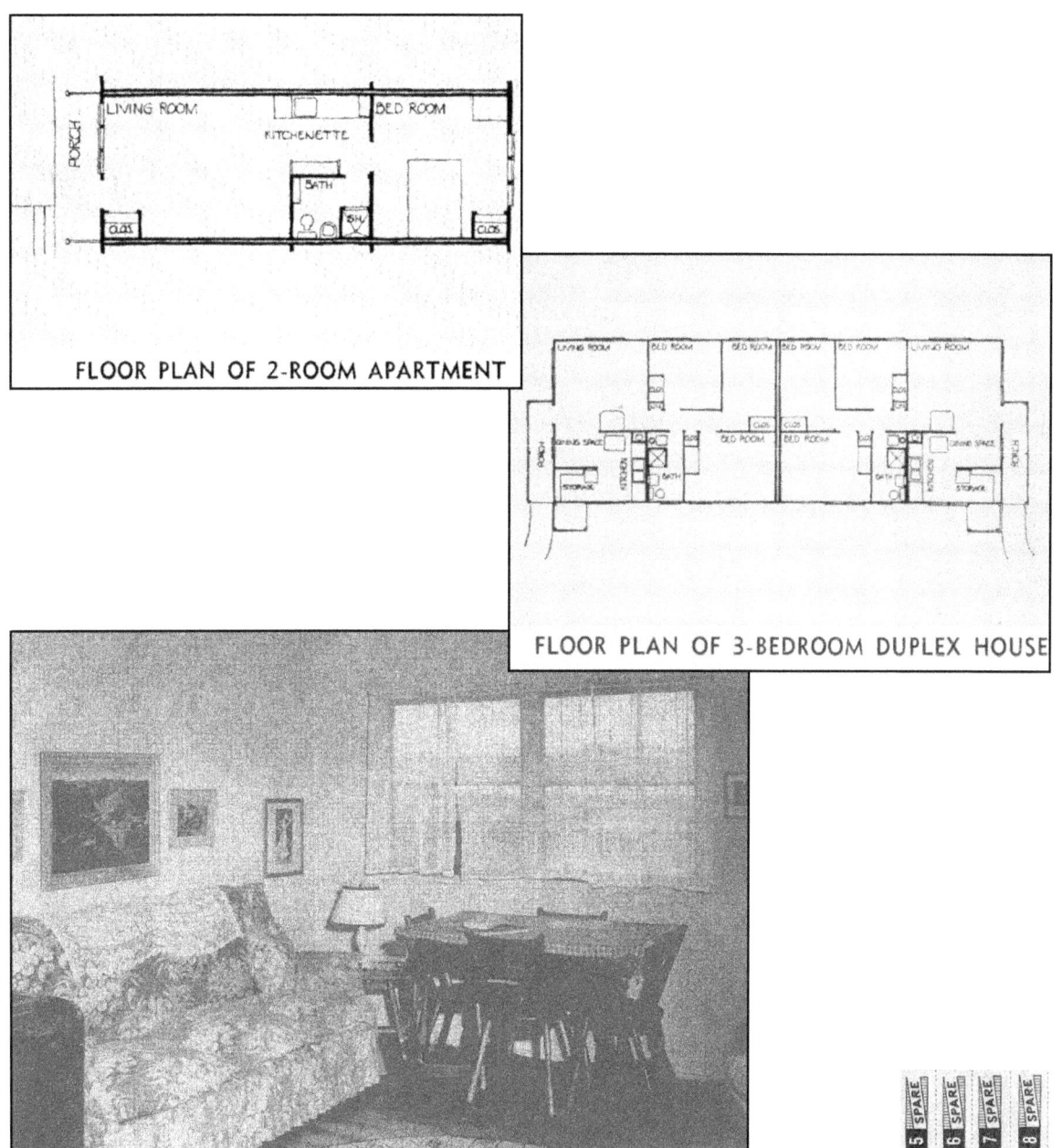

FLOOR PLAN OF 2-ROOM APARTMENT

FLOOR PLAN OF 3-BEDROOM DUPLEX HOUSE

Marin City Memories

Market

The stores in Marin City were built on flat land, and when it rained, everything was flooded. You would practically have to row a boat to get to the stores.

—Levy Bradley

Marin City Memories

Thing's has changed at lot since then. Even the weather has changed. When I first came here, it was so foggy and cold. I just could not believe my eyes. When it came August in Louisiana, it was hot and humid, but here it was cold. I would get on the bus to go to San Rafael with a jacket and get to San Rafael, and it was hot. And then when I came back here, I would have to put my jacket on. That was one thing that really stood out in my mind, how different the weather was from one little place to the other, where in Louisiana it was hot here, it was hot everywhere.

—Helen May

Other workers -Jim & Octavia Harris - Walter Lee, Sr

Marin City Memories

There were no differences of feelings; no racism. We all lived together.

— Rev. Leon Samuels

Oh, we loved it. I mean, as a kid, what do you know? It was duplex housing. Then they started tearing places down and moving and rebuilding. I went to Marin City School. The children in Marin City went to schoo in Marin City, Black and White. It was totally integrated at that time.

— Betty Times

Marin City Memories

Marin City Post Office

They never built the Post Office back. They never built nothing back but one little store, and they opened one of the buildings that people used to live in for the cleaners (Mr. C.J. Williams) and for the cafeteria (Smitty) and for the beauty shop and the barber shop and a little pool room on the end.
— Wilma Hall

Other workers-Dennis McElroy-Harman McKee-Willie Smith,Sr.

Marin City Memories

Shoppers lined up for a sale at the market

We had a drug store, we had a candy store, we had a variety store, we had a cleaners, we had a beauty shop, we had barber shop, we had a big supermarket, we had a cafeteria, and we had a clinic. We had a post office. You could go up there to the doctor. All of that was here when we came.

Then they started tearing down and moving things. I've seen Marin City built three times.

—Wilma Hall

We had a ball diamond right down there too. They had ball games down there. Every Saturday evening and through the week, they would be playing ball down there, right here where the shopping center is now. Me and my husband were going together at the time, and we would sit out there in the stand and watch them play ball.

—Nora Lee Condra

Marin City Memories

The wind was blowing, and you had to wear bandanas. The weather was bad. We bought boots, knee-high boots, to get out to the bus station. It rained. It just rained. Oh, it was terrible. It rained so many days and so many nights. I went to work in the rain, I worked in the rain, I came home in the rain. I got up the next day and went back to work in the rain. Oh, it was bad. It was just like that ocean over there.

—Mary Peoples

Entrepreneurs - Beauty Salon - Juanita Anderson - Nancy Best

Marin City Memories

After the war time housing was torn down, we didn't have anything. It was just the houses, and that was it. There was one little Mom and Pop store which was called Hayden's Store with bread, milk. Just things like that. You'd have to go to the supermarket to shop.

It was left with much of nothing but the housing and that was it. It seemed so destructive to me when they tore down the houses. They just took a bulldozer and just crushed it. I'd never seen that done. Growing up in a culture where people didn't have a lot of houses, I just thought it was pretty destructive.

— Helen May

Pool Hall/Shoe Shine Stand - Moses Beard - Beauty Salon - Eddie Mae Brown

Marin City Memories

Well, it was much different because everyone here were neighbors. We all knew one another. We looked out for one another, the children and the houses. When the ice man came, we could leave the money and leave our doors open. We could leave the money for him. If it rained, and you were out somewhere, your neighbor would take your clothes in for you and put them in the house.
—Beatrice Johnson

Marin City Memories

If I dared do anything wrong, my mother knew about it real quick. Everybody was concerned about each other's kids, and there was a lot of communication back and forth.

—Doug Quiett

Marin City Memories

During the war and right after the war, we had Housing Authority functions for some recreation. Later on, we got parents organized. I had an old station wagon at the time. I used to drive kids from my church to other places. A lot of other people were doing the same thing. So we did a lot of things, just freely giving our time. As a result of that, we had a good group of kids in the area at that particular time.

They did well in school, and it was a pleasure to work with the kids, you know. You like to see a kid develop to their fullest potential.

— James Quiett

Marin City Memories

Marin City Memories

We moved into one of the wartime houses. They were very comfortable. The only thing I disliked was the kerosene stoves. They were very smoky and dirty. You had a kerosene tank on the back of the stove. You had a little round tank, and you had to fill that with kerosene…You'd have to light the eye with a match and then shake the little top on it until it got going. They smoked a lot, and you had a hard time keeping anything around it clean because of the smoke.

—Helen May

Dry Goods & Department Store - Daniel Hayden

Marin City Memories

Where Hayden's Market was, they called it "The Front." We used to say, "Hey baby, I'll see you at The Front." It was a meeting place. We'd sit down there and talk out in front of the Market in those days.

— James Mims

Taxi Stand - Lindsay Cage - Frank Gray - Charlie Hall

Marin City Memories

Marin County was really prejudiced to a certain degree. Blacks couldn't rent outside of Marin City. You couldn't buy a lot. You couldn't buy a place nowhere. In 1947 two fellows bought a lot down in Tennessee Valley. They fired the real estate woman the same day that she sold it to them. They got the sale, and they built later, but she was fired for selling to Blacks.

—Frank Phillips

Food Truck - Rev. Loverd Howard - Gas & Oil Station - Mitchell Howard

Marin City Memories

They wouldn't sell to Blacks anywhere in the county. We just stayed in the old war housing. When the war was over, I guess people thought we'd go back where we came from.

—Flossie Berry

Cafeteria - Henry Morris - Taxi Cab - Neal- Barber Shop - Louis Pickens

Marin City Memories

After the shipyard days, people became afraid that the temporary housing would be torn down, and and we would have to move. We organized a committee that was watching what was happening to the temporary housing projects in other areas, and we heard that people were being evicted over in Berkeley and went over there to see what was happening. WE MADE UP OUT MINDS RIGHT THEN THAT NOTHING LIKE THAT WOULD EVER HAPPEN IN MARIN CITY. WE WOULD NEVER LET PEOPLE BE EVICTED IN MASS FROM THIS COMMUNITY.

—Jesse Berry

Candy Store - Leroy Spigner - Meat Market - Hardy Westmore

Marin City Memories

The housing was so difficult for minorities in the Bay Area, because nobody was building anything for minorities. And this was it. And when we got developers down here, we'd say, "Are you going to build anything for minorities?" "No, we kind of thought they'd move on."

We were trapped. You couldn't move anywhere. Of course, quite a few people did move out. Not in Marin County, but some of them moved to Oakland, Berkeley, San Francisco, Palo Alto, Menlo Park, East Palo Alto. A lot of minority people from this area moved out.

—James Quiett

Cleaners - C.J. Williams - Theo Barron - Shoe Repair - San Rafael

Marin City Memories

The Tenant's Council was one of the things that saved Marin City because after the war we were negotiating to build permanent homes here in Marin City. It was a pretty hard deal. One guy offered a million dollars to build a park and eliminate all the houses. That didn't come through. We had a committee, and we fought to see that the housing was replaced.

I was pretty active. We had 13 members, integrated. We had about six White and the rest Blacks. So we worked together to solve the problems. We went to Washington to save Marin City and got Congressmen involved and the Supervisors, so in about '58 they organized the Redevelopment Agency and the Housing Commission. That was the end that we were working towards seeing that we got justice.

—Frank Phillips

Thurman Barnes - Automobile Repair - San Rafael

Marin City Memories

The State code for pole houses was that you put it on a concrete pad and up above ground, concrete. That didn't happen over here initially, I understand. They just had them on a concrete pad and sand around it. So that was somewhat of a violation of the State code.

Now the ones they built on Buckelew ... the concrete came up above the ground level, and it worked out that that was meeting the requirement there. Those poles were supposed to last at least fifty years, but they're still going. They were impregnated with some kind of chemical that preserved them.

—James Quiett

It wasn't part of the master plan at all. They came up with the Scheuer plan. That's how the pole housing came in.

They got Barrett's Construction Company to do the construction and put them up. I'd go to work and come back, and there'd be a house up. All they'd do is set the poles in the ground, bring them in prefab and set them in.

—Frank Phillips

Marin City Memories

The pole houses are very comfortable. A lot of people liked them, and a lot of people didn't. I didn't like mine when I first seen it going up, but as it was being built, I watched them put it together, and it is well put together. When earthquakes come, nothing falls in your house. Nothing. The looks didn't look good to a lot of people, but I love my house.

—Wilma Hall

Where this house is situated, it was just a mud puddle. My mother used to call it a duck pond. I can remember one day I brought her by to show her where the house was going, and she said, "Baby, you'll never be able to put a house there." But we finally got a house here, and we drove the ducks away (laughs).

—Thelma McKinney

Evelyn "Tootsie" Williams - Beauty Salon - Mill Valley

Marin City Memories

We got Proposition C passed to build 300 units of public housing. We got that approved by the county. They put it on the ballot to get the approval to build 300 units on this property. We failed on 500 units scattered throughout the county. They voted that out. They didn't pass that. See, if they had approved that, you would have had scattered houses all over the county. Well, poor people could have been living there and not congested in one area.

—Frank Phillips

Billy "PeeWee" Thomas - Auto Detailing - San Rafael

Marin City Memories

Mr. Janis

Lincoln Simpson

George Coleman

Marin City Memories

C.J. and Ola Johnson

Mary Peoples
"Momma Mary"

Louise Page

Marin City Memories

Annie Small

Wilma Hall

Marin City Memories

Sedonia Givens

Jesse Berry

Louise McMichael

Moses Beard

Marin City Memories

All of the ladies that live by the hill we've been knowing each other and all of us got children and all of us got grandchildren and all of us got people that know each other from time back. It's beautiful. It is very special to me.

—Wilma Hall

Marin City Memories

The Grandparents Support Group

I have lived in Marin City for the longest time, and I will continue to live here until I die. There is no place that I'd rather stay.

—Maebelle Williams

Marin City Memories

Ben Myles

Flossie Berry

Nora Lee Condra

Marin City Memories

Theo Barron

Robert Thomas
"Pieman"

Alvin Allen

Marin City Memories

Ira McIntosh

Levy Bradley

James Quiett

Annie Small

Marin City Memories

Marguerita C. Johnson

A retired teacher and librarian, Ms. Johnson served as chairwoman of the Marin Area Agency on Aging and was an elected member of the Marin City Community Services District, Marin City Community Development Corporation and Sausalito School District.

She advocated for the construction of the senior center, meal programs and improved in-home services to enable frail elderly to remain in their homes with their loved ones.

Acknowledgements

Marin City Elders:
Nora Lee Condra
Wilma Hall
Beatrice Johnson
Helen May
Thelma McKinney
James Mims
Mary Peoples
Frank Phillips
James Quiett

Marie Gaines
Marguerita C. Johnson Senior Center

Jocelyn Moss
David Dodd
Anne Kent California History Room
Marin County Free Library

Merry Alberigi
Jocelyn Moss
Lynn Skillings
Christopher Edgerton
Marin History Museum

Liz Robinson
Wallace Shephard
John Pullin
Marinship Exhibit
S.F. Bay Model

Evertt Heynneman
Sausalito Historical Society

Susan Goldstein
San Francisco History Room
San Francisco Public Library

Partially funded by
the Marin Arts Council

Marin City Memories

Emme Fisk Gilman, photographer, conservationist and public health educator, photographed Marin City as it was transformed by redevelopment in the early 1960's. Emme photographed Marin City residents living in the deteriorated wartime housing and those same residents after they had moved into the newly constructed pole houses. Her before and after portraits show Marin City undergoing massive physical change. Ms. Gilman died at age 98 in 1997.

Nita Winter, a Marin City based, award winning photographer, has fine art images in corporate exhibits, fine art galleries and private collections locally and nationally. Her projects have included "The Children of the Tenderloin," the book Changing the Odds, Middle School Reform in Progress, Glide Church's poetry booklet Singing Your Own Song, and her annual illustration of the Children's Defense Fund calendars.

In Ms. Winter's project, "The Faces of Marin City," she worked closely with the community to create a series of portraits and text illustrating the diversity, history and sense of community spirit and pride in Marin City. She has continued the series with "The Faces of Novato" and is currently working on "The Faces of..." projects for other Bay Area communities.

Marilyn Geary first discovered oral history in 1977 when she interviewed Sicilian fishermen on San Francisco's Fisherman's Wharf. She has since conducted oral histories for the Save Our Stories Oral History Project of the Alliance for American Quilts, for the Mill Valley Historical Society, and for the Faces of Marin City Project. She has most recently documented San Francisco's Madonna del Lume Celebration and the Blessing of the Fishing Fleet for the Library of Congress Bicentennial Local Legacy Program. Marilyn is on the Board of Directors of the Mill Valley Historical Society and is editor of the Society's website and newsletter. She is a member of the Association of Personal Historians, the Oral History Association, and the Bay Area Oral Historians Group.

Marin City Memories

Sources

Photographs of Emme Fisk Gilman
The Anne Kent California History Room
Marin County Free Library
Pages 44, 51, 53, 55, 57, 59, 61, 65, 67, 80, 82

Marin City 1942, Revisited
Pages 6, 10, 21, 26, 27, 30, 56, 58

Marin History Museum
Outside cover, preface, pages 1, 2, 3, 7, 9, 11, 13, 15, 16, 19, 20, 23, 34, 68

Marin Housing Authority
Pages 4, 33, 34, 36, 37, 38, 39, 40, 41, 63, 69

Photographs of Nita Winter
Pages 75, 76, 77, 78

Private Albums and Collections
Pages 25, 43, 46, 47, 48, 49, 70, 71, 72, 73, 74, 79

San Francisco History Room
San Francisco Public Library
Pages 29, 32, 35, 42, 63, 64, 66

Marinship Exhibit
S.F. Bay Model Visitor Center
Sausalito Historical Society
Pages 24, 26, 27, 28, 30, 31, 38

For additional copies: www.marilynlgeary.com/marin-city-memories/